Sustainability in the Public Sector

An Essential Briefing for Stakeholders

Sonja Powell

Founder Director of the Sustainable Development Bureau &
Director of the Global Association of Corporate Sustainability Officers
(GACSO)

First published in 2013 by Dō Sustainability
87 Lonsdale Road, Oxford OX2 7ET, UK

ISBN 978-1-909293-31-1 (eBook-ePub)
ISBN 978-1-909293-32-8 (eBook-PDF)
ISBN 978-1-909293-30-4 (Paperback)

A catalogue record for this title is available from the British Library.

Dō Sustainability strives for net positive social and environmental impact.
See our sustainability policy at **www.dosustainability.com**.

Page design and typesetting by Alison Rayner
Cover by Becky Chilcott

For further information on Dō Sustainability, visit our website:
www.dosustainability.com

DōShorts

Dō Sustainability is the publisher of **DōShorts**: short, high-value ebooks that distil sustainability best practice and business insights for busy, results-driven professionals. Each DōShort can be read in 90 minutes.

New and forthcoming DōShorts – stay up to date

We publish 3 to 5 new DōShorts each month. The best way to keep up to date? Sign up to our short, monthly newsletter. Go to **www.dosustainability.com/newsletter** to sign up to the Dō Newsletter. Some of our latest and forthcoming titles include:

- *Green Jujitsu: Embed Sustainability into Your Organisation*
  Gareth Kane

- *How to Make your Company a Recognised Sustainability Champion*   Brendan May

- *Making the Most of Standards* Adrian Henriques

- *Promoting Sustainable Behaviour: A Practical Guide to What Works*   Adam Corner

- *How to Account for Sustainability*   Laura Musikanski

- *Sustainability in the Public Sector*   Sonja Powell

- *Sustainability Reporting for SMEs*   Elaine Cohen

- *Sustainable Transport Fuels Business Briefing*   David Thorpe

- *The Changing Profile of Corporate Climate Change Risk*
  Mark Trexler & Laura Kosloff

- *The First 100 Days: Plan, Prioritise & Build a Sustainable Organisation*   Anne Augustine

- *The Short Guide to Sustainable Investing*   Cary Krosinsky

- *REDD+ and Business Sustainability*   Brian McFarland

Subscriptions

In additional to individual sales and rentals, we offer individual and organisational subscriptions to our full collection of published and forthcoming books. To discuss a subscription for yourself or your organisation, email **veruschka@dosustainability.com**

Write for us, or suggest a DōShort

Please visit **www.dosustainability.com** for our full publishing programme. If you don't find what you need, write for us! Or Suggest a DōShort on our website. We look forward to hearing from you.

....

Abstract

THE SINGLE MOST IMPORTANT ACTION to support a sustainable future in terms of democratic decision-making is to build a widespread grounding in basic sustainability understanding. This will help to develop motivation for urgent action, through better understanding of the damage being caused by current unsustainable practices. Many people are not sure what is meant by the phase 'sustainable development'. This book begins by uncovering the history of the term 'sustainable development' and introduces basic sustainability theory. Unsustainable practices are exposed and the disastrous consequences of 'carrying on as normal' highlighted. Realities of the politics behind this agenda are laid bare alongside the responses of successive political administrations. Finally, a snapshot of sustainable development in local government is developed and the roadmap for achieving the UK's 2050 carbon reduction targets demystified. The book will be invaluable to a variety of public bodies, such as local authorities, and their stakeholders, including councillors, officers, members of Local Enterprise Partnerships, Local Nature Partnerships, scrutiny panels and other forums, in enhancing understanding of both the sustainable development challenge facing us today and the political backdrop to this agenda.

....

About the Author

SONJA POWELL has cultivated a working knowledge of local and central government from 20 years spent developing and implementing economic and social policy. In 2010, Sonja added 'environmental' to her 'economic' and 'social' experience by graduating with an MBA from Nottingham University, host to the International Centre for Corporate Social Responsibility (ICCSR). While completing her thesis, Sonja worked in association with the award-winning sustainability charity Forum for the Future within their Public Sector Hub and received recommendations from Sara Parking OBE and Jonathon Porritt CBE.

Sonja is Founder Director of the Sustainable Development Bureau, specialising in capacity–building, including stakeholder sustainability planning, engagement and implementation. She undertook research with many leading organisations and sustainability figures to investigate the feasibility of a movement supporting ethical and sustainable products and services, and hosted two four-day residential congresses at the 2011 Findhorn International Congresses on Sustainability, attended by high-profile professionals.

Sonja is also Director of the Global Association of Corporate Sustainability Officers (GACSO) and blogs on sustainability for The UK carbon reduction network, E2B Pulse.

Who is This Book For?

THIS 90-MINUTE READ provides a solid introduction to sustainability in the public sector. It is intended to equip the reader with background knowledge and understanding of the fundamental issues. This includes:

1. *Counsellors, community and business leaders, and local authority officers*, who need to be equipped for decision-making; sustainability and climate change is the critical factor to be taken into consideration when making decisions. This ebook provides both an understanding of the sustainable development challenge facing us today and the political perspective.

2. *Sustainability leads*, in the search to uncover those actions which make the biggest impact towards ingraining sustainability in the public sector.

3. *Aspiring candidates*, seeking positions or promotion within sustainability teams; provides background knowledge to assist with a successful interview.

4. *Students* of public administration.

....

Contents

CHAPTER 1

Understanding the Issues

Sustainable development means meeting the needs of the present, without compromising the ability of future generations to meet theirs.

(Brundtland Report, 1989)

THIS CHAPTER PROVIDES ESSENTIAL background knowledge, introducing the reader to the field of sustainable development. The first step is to build common understanding of what is meant by the term 'sustainable development' through uncovering the history of the term and introducing basic sustainability theory. This leads the way to considering the scope of the challenge faced, which is achieved by highlighting current unsustainable practices.

What is sustainable development?

Many people are unsure what is meant by the phase 'sustainable development'. One reason for this is the scope of the topic; it is wide-ranging and it is often necessary to check what aspect of sustainability is being referred to. The terms 'sustainability' and 'sustainable development', which are used interchangeably in this book, mean meeting the needs of the present without compromising the ability of future generations to meet theirs. To support a fuller understanding, the background to the term 'sustainability' is provided below, followed by an introduction to sustainability theory and how it differs from economic theory.

Dyllick and Hockerts (2002) offer a history to the term 'sustainability' and its dimensions. It has emerged from distinct stakeholder groups as follows:

1972: **Ecologists** constructed sustainability as a concept concerned with the *protection of the environment*. The United Nations Conference on the Human Environment (in Stockholm), called on states and international organizations to "play a co-ordinated, efficient and dynamic role for the protection and improvement of the environment".

1970s onwards: **Business strategy scholars** searched for *sustainable competitive advantage*.

1987: **The Brundtland Commission** emphasised the link between the economic plight of developing countries and sustainable development. They defined *sustainable development* as: *'meeting the needs of the present, without compromising the ability of future generations to meet theirs'*.

1990s: **United Nations** conferences in the 1990s added the notion of *social sustainability* in debates on education for all, human rights, population and development, women, and social development.

Sustainability theory

Three emerging dimensions arise from the above history. These are illustrated in the 'triple bottom line' which is made up of the environmental case, the social case, and the business case for sustainability. Figure 1 is an illustration of the three dimensions of sustainability. Elkington's model below is both easy to understand and widely used.

....

FIGURE 1. The three dimensions of sustainability, known as the triple bottom line.

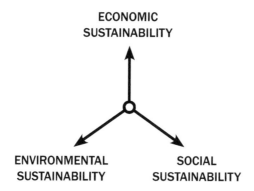

SOURCE: Dyllick and Hockerts (2002) and Elkington (1997).

....

'Triple bottom line' is now standard sustainability theory and illustrates that the financial or 'single bottom line' traditionally used by organisations is insufficient for overall sustainability. The overemphasis on short-term economic gain has largely ignored longer-term costs caused by social and environmental damage.

In economic theory, 'burned soil' (where natural and social resources have been depleted without much concern for potential future costs) represents externalities or market failure. Long-term economic sustainability is threatened by the burned soil effect. An example of this effect is provided in Figure 2, which shows global carbon emissions from fossil fuel burning between 1751 and 2010. It illustrates that since the Industrial Revolution there has been a dramatic increase in carbon emissions.

FIGURE 2. Global carbon emissions from fossil fuel burning.

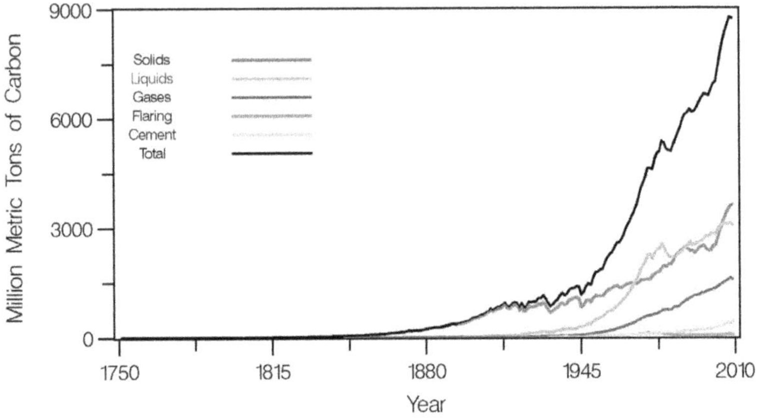

SOURCE: Carbon Dioxide Information Analysis Center (CDIAC).

The solution is for organisations, already used to maintaining their economic capital base, to also manage their natural and social capital in order to achieve long-term sustainability. In economic models the role of government is to correct market failure, suggesting that government should be acting to correct and prevent unsustainable development by supporting organisations in their management of all three types of capital which make up the triple bottom line.

Clarity on the three types of capital is provided by Dyllick and Hockerts (2002) as follows:

- *Economic capital*: economic sustainability requires the manage-ment of several types of capital – *financial capital* (i.e. equity and debt); *tangible capital* (i.e. machinery, land and stocks) and *intangible capital* (i.e. reputation, inventions, know-how, organisational routines).

- **Natural capital**: this includes *natural resources* in renewable form (i.e. wood, fish, corn) and non-renewable form (i.e. fossil fuel, biodiversity, social quality); and *ecosystem resources* (i.e. climate stabilisation, water purification, soil remediation, reproduction of plants and animals).

- **Social capital**: this is divided into *human capital* (i.e. skills, motivation, and loyalty of staff and business partners); and *societal capital* (i.e. quality of public services like education, infrastructure, culture supportive of entrepreneurship).

In managing economic capital, different types of capital can be substituted. However, many forms of social and natural capital cannot be replaced by economic capital. We cannot for example substitute the ozone layer with other resources. Additionally, many capital types complement each other and are multi-functional, for example, forests and oceans act as sinks that absorb, neutralise or recycle wastes; forests also provide wood, paper, etc. and habitats for biodiversity. Finally, there are ethical considerations; even if no financial value has been put on a particular species, are we not morally and ethically required to protect it? Biodiversity is being lost at an alarming rate; when we lose a species this is irreversible.

Unsustainable development

We have seen that the global ecosystem is finite and fixed, and that economic activity transforms natural products into wastes that nature must then absorb. Nature's capacity to absorb wastes is now being pushed to, and in some cases well beyond, its limits. Sara Parkin (2010) refers to five 'symptoms' of unsustainable development caused by current practices. These are summarised below (facts and figures used here provide a macro-picture; local statistics could be compiled for a micro-perspective):

1. *Persistent poverty, injustice and inequality of opportunity for many people.* The number of people classed as living in extreme poverty, defined as living on less than $1.25 per day, is 1.29 billion or approximately 22% of the world population (World Bank Development Research Group, 2012). A quarter of children are undernourished. UNHCR 2011 statistics show rising numbers of people forcibly displaced worldwide at 43.7m people, the highest number in 15 years, with the number of refugees at 15.4 million to the end of 2009.

   The next symptom of unsustainable development points to competition for scarce resources as an increasingly important factor in provoking and perpetuating violence, one of the drivers behind these statistics.

2. *Mineral depletion including platinum, phosphorus, nickel, lead, indium, gold, copper, zinc, silver, aluminium, uranium, chromium, etc.:* Many minerals are already in short supply or hard to extract; extraction also adds to CO_2 emissions. Minerals are used in everyday items such as digital and telecommunications and renewable energy technologies. Stocks of fossil fuels including coal and oil are also diminishing. Parkin (2010) raises the point that violent conflicts over mineral resources are on the increase

(the conflicts in eastern Congo, where fighting has continued over 15 years driven by the trade in valuable minerals, are an example) and part of an overall picture of shortages of non-biological and therefore non-renewable resources worldwide.

3. *Biological resource depletion including minerals, oil, water, soil fertility, forests, grass and wetlands.* The 2005 Millennium Eco-system Assessment (MEA) on the state of the global environment found that 15 of 24 ecosystem services (60%) are being degraded or used unsustainably, including fresh drinking water.

Changes in ecosystems due to human activity have been more rapid and extensive in the last 50 years than in any comparable period of time. Resources have been used to meet rapidly growing demand for food, fresh water, timber, fibre and fuel. This activity has contributed to substantial gains in human well-being and economic development. However, it has also resulted in a significant and often irreversible loss of the diversity of life on Earth. If the problems are not addressed now, future generations will experience a sizeable loss in benefits from ecosystems. The World Wide Fund for Nature calculates that we are exceeding the planet's ability to regenerate by about 30%.

4. *Waste generation.* The natural environment has its own efficient recycling system. However, it is overloaded by alien substances: visible rubbish such as plastic, packaging, rubble, etc. and invisible air and waterborne pollutants including man-made chemicals and fertilisers, excessive CO_2, etc. Consider just one example of waste: plastic bags represent a fraction of 1% of waste generated, but cause much greater damage. Sean Poulter and

David Derbyshire when launching the campaign to banish plastic bags in 2008 highlighted that:

> *Typically they are used for only 20 minutes before being thrown out. But they will take up to 1,000 years to rot away. During their long decay millions linger to pollute our streets, the countryside, parks, rivers and seas. Britain's coast is washed with a toxic 'plastic soup' carried on the tide which threatens our seabirds, turtles, whales and other wildlife. Gannets off Cornwall suffer a long painful death, unable to feed or fly after getting entangled. Dolphins scoop up plastic bags and carry them around, risking strangulation and suffocation. And some 8% of the world's seal population has reportedly been harmed by plastic bags.*

Three other side effects identified by Parkin (2010) from waste generation include:

- A quarter of ill health caused by environmental hazards is due to waste and pollution.

- For each tonne of consumables bought by UK adults, an average of 10 times that weight of material (rock, water, energy, etc.) has to be moved or used to make that purchase possible. It's 540,000 times for gold; expressed another way, 5.4 tonnes of material have to be mined for a wedding ring.

- Roughly 40% of the food we buy we throw away.

Cutting out waste, being thrifty and using fewer resources saves on materials and drastically reduces CO_2 emissions. This is central to a low carbon economy.

5. *Fossil fuel burning*. Small amounts of greenhouse gases are essential; greenhouse gases help retain in the atmosphere enough infrared radiation from the Earth to keep the temperature required for life. CO_2 forms the biggest proportion of the greenhouse gases. Normally CO_2 moves in continual chemical interaction between the air, sea and earth; see Figure 3 for an illustration of the carbon cycle (NASA, Earth Observatory, 2010). However, due to human activity (burning carboniferous fossil fuels, changes to land use

FIGURE 3. The carbon cycle.

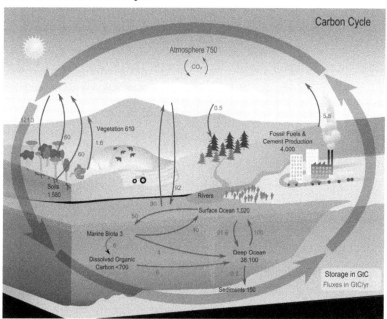

SOURCE: NASA, Earth Observatory (2010).

from deforestation and agriculture) CO_2 and other greenhouse gases in the atmosphere have increased dramatically. The earth and sea components of the global carbon recycling system have become overwhelmed, leaving a growing proportion of the gases in the atmosphere. The unnaturally high levels of greenhouse gases in the atmosphere are causing excessive heating of the Earth's atmosphere; as well as changing the climate it is making the sea more acidic. Climate change is a symptom of unsustainable development.

A few years earlier the Stern Review (2007) reported similar findings. The report explained that:

Scientific evidence suggests that the stocks of greenhouse gases in the atmosphere (including carbon dioxide, methane, nitrous oxides and a number of gases that arise from industrial processes) are rising, as a result of human activity.

The report stated that in 2005 the stock of greenhouse gases in the atmosphere was equivalent to around 430 parts per million (ppm) CO_2, compared to 280 ppm before the Industrial Revolution. These concentrations have caused the world to warm by more than half a degree Celsius and would lead to at least a further half a degree warming over the next few decades. It went on to say that the annual flow of emissions is accelerating and unabated there was likely to be a global average temperature rise exceeding 2% by 2035, and a 5% rise in the subsequent century. We are now only 5 degrees Celsius warmer than the last Ice Age, and such changes would transform the physical geography of the world.

The Stern Review (2007: vi–viii) warned of disastrous consequences if action is not taken to mitigate the effects of climate change. Three of their headline findings were:

- *Climate change threatens the basic elements of life* for people around the world – access to water, food production, health, and use of land and the environment. Severe impacts included: reduced water supplies threatening one-sixth of the world population; declining crop yields leaving millions without the ability to produce or purchase sufficient food; increases in deaths from cold, heat, malnutrition and diseases; flooding and droughts; and around 15–40% of species potentially facing extinction after only 2 degrees Celsius of warming.

- *The damage from climate change will accelerate* as the world gets warmer: this could take the world outside the range of human experience.

- *The poorest countries would suffer earliest and most* and if and when the damage appears it will be too late to reverse the process; thus we are forced to look a long way ahead.

The recommendation of the Stern Review was that the benefits of strong, early action considerably outweigh the costs. They estimated that the impact of uncontrolled climate change would be like losing up to 20% of world GDP now and forever in the future; however, stabilising greenhouse gas concentrations would cost around 2–3% of global GDP. Mitigation must be viewed as an investment to avoid the risks of very serious consequences in the future: 'policy must promote sound market signals, overcome market failures and have equity and risk mitigation at its core'.

In 2009, the senior economist on the team that produced the Stern Review, Alex Bowen said that 'the Review was based on science available up to 2005; revisions of the impact of unrestrained climate change would be substantially higher'.

Parkin and Stern have painted a bleak picture of the consequences of unsustainable development. Parkin has pointed to: depletion of biological resources on which life depends and depletion of mineral resources central to modern life; an irreversible loss of diversity of life and substantial loss of ecosystems; increased waste and increasing ill health from the resulting pollution; poverty and an increase in wars and violent conflict resulting from scarcity; and finally, increasing greenhouse gas emissions creating climate change as a result of exponential increases in resource use. On top of all this the global population is set to almost double by 2050.

Only 50 years ago the world population was 3 billion people. Today it is 7 billion and projected to grow to 9 billion by 2050 (Rees, 2010). Whilst the UK population is projected to increase by 10 million by 2033, the majority of the population growth is in the developing world. An example is India's population, which is expected to overtake China's and reach 1.5 billion, and there could be a billion more people in Africa in 2050 than there are today. This will magnify current struggles around providing clean water, sufficient food and preventing soil degradation. The debate on population growth merits particular focus on the oppression and marginalisation of women, especially in the third world, and the causal relationship held. The scientist and author Vandana Shiva (2002) examined this topic in detail.

Martin Rees draws two main conclusions with regard to population growth: first, there needs to be enhanced education and empowerment for women; and second, a higher population would aggravate all pressures on resources – especially if the developing world narrows the gap with the developed world in per capita consumption. Debates around population are both sensitive and political. In the UK, for example, about a third of pregnancies are unplanned and this offers potential for political initiatives to provide free contraception.

Clearly, the solutions to all the issues raised include government action. The politics of sustainable development is discussed in the next chapter.

....

CHAPTER 2

The Politics of Sustainable Development

The myth of growth has failed us. It has failed the two billion people who still live on less than $2 a day. It has failed the fragile ecological systems on which we depend for survival. It has failed, spectacularly, in its own terms, to provide economic stability and secure peoples livelihoods.

(Tim Jackson, *Prosperity Without Growth? The Transition to a Sustainable Economy*, 2009: 3)

IT IS EVIDENT FROM THE CONSEQUENCES of unsustainable development detailed in Chapter 1 that we cannot go on as we have been. Environmentalists have been sending out warnings about unsustainable development since the 1960s, for example, Rachel Carsons's famous book *Silent Spring* (1962), and influential people have long been aware of the problem, thus the question has to be asked, why has so little been done about it? This chapter suggests answers to that question by introducing political challenges that lie in the way of a sustainable and low-carbon future.

Why has so little been done to prevent unsustainable development?

As with many matters, it's complicated. Highlighted here are five political challenges which have to be faced. They are as follows:

- Economic and political structures.

- Economic protection.

- The need to maintain secure and efficient energy supplies.

- How to gain and maintain public support for political measures.

- How to protect the vulnerable and the less well-off.

Economic and political structures

Economic growth and success has been built on using more and more energy and resources to produce more and more goods and services. By implication the world's richest nations are also the highest polluters. Emerging nations who are producing more and becoming increasingly wealthy themselves such as India and China show a progressively upward emissions trend. This correlation is illustrated by comparing regional positions on the two charts below. Figure 4 shows carbon dioxide emissions by region; Figure 5 gives GDP by region.

Comparing the charts between 1990 and 2010, we can see that Africa and Brazil have low GDP and low CO_2 emissions. OECD Europe and America have high CO_2 emissions and high GDP. China merits special mention, as it is growing at a rapid pace; for example, there are 17,000 kilometers of high-speed railways under construction in China, the longest in the world. China is also increasing the number of airports from the current 180 in 2012 to 230 by 2015, with a combined capacity of 450 million passengers a year. China's airlines are expected to have a combined fleet of 4500 airplanes by 2015. In 2006 China's emissions exceeded those of the US for the first time; likewise its GDP shows a

....

FIGURE 4. World carbon dioxide emissions.

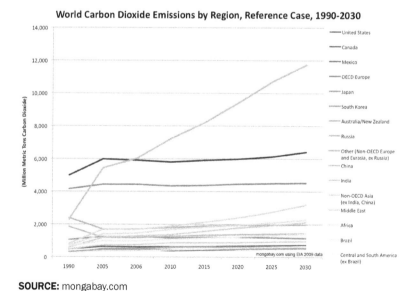

SOURCE: mongabay.com

....

....

FIGURE 5. World GDP.

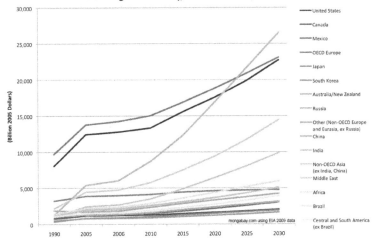

World Gross Domestic Product (GDP) by Region Expressed in
Purchasing Power Parity, Reference Case, 1990-2030

SOURCE: mongabay.com

....

sharp rise from 2006. China's GDP is expected to overtake US GDP in the next 10 years and become the world's richest nation.

As the correlation between the charts illustrate, the first challenge is the economic system and how to decouple economic growth from consumption? Prugh et al. (2000) pointed out that present-day Americans consume 30% of the world's non-renewable resources, with only 6% of the world's population. The Rees Lectures (2010) took this point further saying that:

> The world couldn't sustain anywhere near its current population if everyone lived like present day Americans. On the other hand, more

than 10 billion people could live sustainably, with a high quality of life, if all adopted a vegetarian diet, travelling little but interacting just via super internet and virtual reality.

The task of unravelling economic growth and consumption is not easy. According to Parkin (2010) vested interests in the current economic system is one reason for legislation concentrating on 'end of pipe' pollution and waste (i.e. legislation around emissions: setting limits, selling permits; monitoring these; and enforcing these) rather than government focusing its attentions on preventing the use of resources and waste generation in the first place.

Authors such as F.C. Matthes (2009) advocate that tackling unsustainable development and climate change necessitates an increased role for the state with more state planning and intervention. This increased state role would need to be legitimised by a clear definition of the challenges to be overcome.

Economic protection

The second political difficulty to be faced is linked to the first. We have seen that, generally speaking, richer countries are higher polluters and countries want to protect or improve their economic positions. In international negotiations countries are aware of the global power-shifting potential of any agreement to cut emissions. This was the main reason behind the Bush administration rejecting the Kyoto Agreement, an international agreement to limit emissions. Even under President Obama, who supports moves to cut carbon emissions, the US is having difficulty getting legislation passed; the 2010 Climate Bill collapsed. The significance of this is that, as the world's richest nation, the rest of the world is watching to see if they can both retain their economic position and cut carbon. So far the message has not been positive. For example, China says it has taken some strong measures to cut carbon; however, it needs energy to support the rapid industrialisation and urbanisation currently underway. If the US is not willing to risk growth to support carbon reductions, why should they? The message from developing countries is that they are willing to tackle emissions in exchange for assistance with low carbon technologies and financing.

The need to maintain secure and efficient energy supplies

A third dilemma is whether energy security is consistent with a low carbon future. Energy is on the political agenda due to a number of other threats including: lack of investment in infrastructure; disruption in fossil fuel supplies; and terrorism. However, it is being flagged up here because of the potential disruption to energy supplies from moving to a dependence on renewable sources of energy.

How to gain and maintain public support for political measures

The fourth issue is how to mobilise and maintain political support for actions required to become sustainable. It is anticipated that the transition to a sustainable and low carbon future will involve a rise in the cost of living. Resource and fuel prices need to rise to reflect their real cost; that is, the cost of externalities needs to be built in. Then there is the cost of industrial re-structuring as we move away from unsustainable practices to a green economy. However, the tensions for politicians and political parties between these difficult long-term issues and the short-term goal of re-election may mean that these issues are dodged. The success of future climate change policy depends both on political strategies for building public support for emissions curbing measures as well as the policy instruments to achieve this.

How to protect the vulnerable and the less well-off

The final issue being raised here deals with the challenge of how to protect the vulnerable and the less well-off. Fuel poverty is the term used when a high percentage of an individual's or household's income has to be spent on keeping warm. However, in a low-carbon economy the cost of externalities needs to be built in to fossil fuel costs, causing prices to rise and the poor are disproportionately affected. Policies are needed to help society's most vulnerable adjust to high energy prices.

The above issues provide one explanation for complaints of inconsistent government policy; on the one hand, trying to look green and on the other, supporting industries which generate significant emissions. One such example was the car scrappage scheme in 2010, where the government provided £2000 for scrapping an old car and replacing it with a new one to stimulate the motor industry. Cars create emissions and there was no requirement to replace the old car with an energy efficient car. Another example at the other end of the spectrum was the drastic and sudden cuts to the solar PV feed-in-tariff scheme in 2012. The tariff paid was very generous (unaffordable) and there was widespread agreement that some reduction in the tariff was necessary. However, the unlawful and sudden way in which it was imposed was seen as unfair and damaged confidence in investing in subsidy-dependent technologies, particularly low-carbon energy generation.

The public sector

So far insights have been provided into the term 'sustainable development' and unsustainable practices have been exposed, accentuating the need for governments to act. The politics of sustainable development have been discussed highlighting the political difficulties which have to be overcome. The next step is to consider what contributions the public sector can make to sustainable development and overcoming these political difficulties. It is important to have an understanding of both the contribution they can make and the limits to that contribution.

Over the last 60 years UK public sector spending has been between 35% and 40% of total spending. At the same time the public sector is responsible for significant environmental, social and economic impacts. Finding sustainable solutions would not only be positive for sustainable development, but in the longer term will save money.

Provided below are government facts and figures on the size of the public sector in the UK (2009):

- *Workforce*: local government, education sector and the National Health Service (NHS) employ just over 15% of the workforce, with the figure rising to 20% for the wider public sector.

- *Service delivery*: local authorities deliver a wide range of services covering areas including education, transport, planning, social services, public health, procurement, energy consumption and provision, recreation and leisure, housing, regeneration and environmental stewardship.

- **Carbon emissions**: the schools estate alone is responsible for around 2% of emissions, and 15% can be attributed to the wider public sector.

- **Housing**: local government in England owns more than 1 in 10 houses and collects over 29m tonnes of household waste per year.

- **Meals**: the NHS serves around 800,000 meals a day in hospitals, creating impacts for food production, processing and transportation.

Public value

In addition to the contribution the public sector can make to the environment from its size and purchasing power, public value arguments add weight to the call for the public sector to take a lead in pursuing sustainable development.

G. Kelly et al. (2009) describe public value in these terms:

Public value provides a broader measure than is currently used... covering outcomes, the means used to deliver them as well as trust and legitimacy. It addresses issues such as equality, ethos, and accountability. Current public management practice sometimes fails to consider, understand or manage this full range of factors.

Public value is therefore a broad concept including trust and legitimacy, as well as outcomes and the means to deliver them. The charity Forum for the Future asserts that public sector organisations are vital players in the creation of a sustainable future and that sustainable development offers the most appropriate set of values for the creation and maintenance of public value (Birney et al., 2010). By taking a sustainable approach, local government can create better services for their citizens and customers.

Local government's ability to act is affected by policies set through central government. The next chapter takes a look at the sustainability responses of successive UK administrations.

....

CHAPTER 3

Sustainability Responses of UK Political Administrations

Sustainable development is first and foremost a political issue. It is about priorities, between peoples of the world and between generations. It requires political will and leadership to build awareness of the challenges and support for the solutions. It should be remembered that the first trigger for many in the business world to begin thinking about climate change was Mrs Thatcher's public acknowledgement of the climate change threat in 1988.

(Roger Cowe and Jonathon Porritt, *Government's Business, Enabling Corporate Sustainability*, 2002)

THE CONCEPT OF SUSTAINABLE DEVELOPMENT gained its first major international recognition in 1972 at the United Nations Conference on Environment and Human Development in Stockholm, where the international community agreed that both development and the environment could be managed to mutual benefit. However, it was not until 1992 that world leader's recognised sustainable development as a major challenge. The UK was the first country to develop a sustainable development strategy in 1994. This chapter provides an insight first into the role of UK political administrations in the evolution of UK government structures for sustainable development, before drilling down into the role played by local government.

Detailed below, from 1979 to the current day, are the dates political administrations were in power. Noted underneath are significant relevant events in the sustainable development calendar which occurred under those administrations and an interpretive summary.

Conservatives: 1979–1997

1989 *Local Government Act*: this act made it a primary objective of councils 'to endeavour to achieve the best outcomes for the local community having regard for the long term and cumulative effects of decisions'. In so doing, councils must have regard to a number of facilitating objectives, including 'to promote the social, economic and environmental viability and sustainability of the municipal district'.

1992 *The international community first recognised the need for sustainable development strategies*: at the Rio Earth Summit in 1992, heads of government from around the world adopted Agenda 21, a blueprint for action on sustainable development for the 21st century, which included a call on all countries to develop national sustainable development strategies. Agenda 21 played an instrumental part in initiating sustainable development in local authorities.

1994 *The UK became the first country to publish a Sustainable Development Strategy*: 'Sustainable Development, the UK Strategy'.

In summary, it is in this period that we start to see the beginnings of government recognising the need for a new, more environmentally sound approach to development so as not to result in excessive environmental deterioration or social injustice. The Thatcher government (1979–1990) is noted for less government intervention, but Grayson (2010) suggests big businesses realised that in return for market liberalisation they had to be prepared to act. 'Businesses created a number of organisations to facilitate action and share learning', including Business in the Community (BITC), local enterprise agencies, and education business partnerships. Towards the end of the 1980s the government devolved responsibility for regeneration and skills training from local authorities and government agencies to Training and Enterprise Councils.

At local authority level, Agenda 21 encouraged innovative and creative sustainability ideas. It provided an invaluable learning phase ahead of the mainstreaming which was to come.

Labour: 1997–2010

1997 *Sustainable development became a fundamental objective of the EU.*

Kyoto Protocol adopted: The Kyoto Protocol is a protocol to the United Nations Framework Convention on Climate Change (UNFCCC or FCCC) that set binding obligations on the industrialised countries to reduce their emissions of greenhouse gases. The Kyoto Protocol came into force in 2005.

1998 *Regional Development Agencies (RDAs) Act*: the RDAs had five statutory purposes, one of which was to contribute to sustainable development.

1999 *A revised UK Sustainable Development Strategy was published*: with devolution, the new democratic bodies in Scotland, Wales and Northern Ireland became responsible for creating their own solutions to the challenge of sustainable development and creating their own sustainable development strategy documents. The UK strategy covered England and all non-devolved issues. The common thread was the UK Government and the Devolved Administrations shared framework *One Future – Different Paths: The UK's Shared Framework for Sustainable Development* (http://www.defra.gov.uk/sustainable/government/publications/uk-strategy/framework-for-sd.htm), which set out shared challenges and goals to provide a consistent approach and focus across the UK.

2000 *Sustainable Development Commission (SDC) established*: positioned within Defra, the SDC was created as a non-departmental advisory body. Through advocacy, advice and appraisal, the SDC's role was to help put sustainable development at the heart of government policy.

2001 *EU leaders launched the first EU sustainable development strategy*: the strategy, launched at the Gothenburg Summit, was composed of two main parts. The first proposed objectives and policy measures to tackle a number of key unsustainable trends; the second called for a new approach to policy-making to ensure that the EU's economic, social and environmental policies mutually reinforced each other.

Defra took responsibility for the 'green' parts of the former Department of the Environment, Transport and the Regions: while all Departments share responsibility for making sustainable development a reality, Defra became the lead department, chairing a programme board to oversee delivery of the strategy.

2005 *The EU Emissions Trading Scheme (EU ETS) launched*: the world's first international company-level 'cap-and trade' system of allowances for emitting carbon dioxide and other greenhouse gases.

The current UK Sustainable Development Strategy was launched: *Securing the Future*; this embodied a definition for sustainable develoment as follows:

The goal of sustainable development is to enable all people throughout the world to satisfy their basis needs and enjoy a better quality of life, without compromising the quality of life of future generations.

And five principles illustrated in Figure 6:

....

FIGURE 6. Five principles for sustainable development policy in the UK.

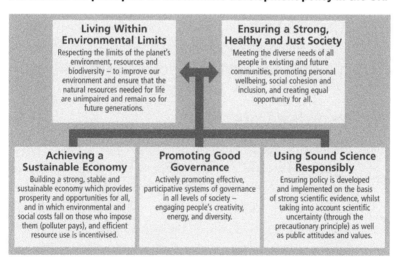

SOURCE: *Securing the Future* (HM Government, 2005).

....

The strategy also strengthened the SDC's role, adding a scrutiny responsibility.

2006 *The EU Sustainable Development Strategy was revised*: recognised the need to change unsustainable consumption and production patterns and move towards a better integrated approach to policy-making. It also documented the importance of strengthening work with partners outside the EU, including those rapidly developing countries that will have a significant impact on global sustainable development such as China.

The Government of Wales Act 2006: made sustainable development an organising principle of government.

> *We remain one of the few administrations in the world to have such a statutory duty and it gives us an opportunity to develop Wales, as a small, smart nation, in ways which contribute sustainability to people's economic, social and environmental wellbeing. (Rt Hon. Rhodi Morgan AM, First Minister for Wales, One Wales: One Planet, 2009)*

2007 *Agenda 21 was disbanded.*

2008 *Creation of the Department of Energy and Climate Change (DECC)*: this brought the UK's energy policy and climate strategy under one roof. Previously the Department for Business, Enterprise and Regulatory Reform (Berr) had responsibility for the nation's energy strategy while the Department for Environment, Food and Rural Affairs (Defra) had the task of trying to curb the rise of greenhouse gases and ensuring energy was used more efficiently.

Climate Change Act: imposed legally binding reductions on CO_2 emissions so that the net UK carbon account for all six Kyoto greenhouse gases for the year 2050 should be at least 80% lower than the 1990 baseline.

2009 *The SDC became an executive non-departmental body*: becoming a Limited Company owned by government, including the devolved administrations, with more freedom to make decisions over staffing and finances. Its remit remained the same.

Comprehensive Performance Assessment: when the new performance framework was introduced in April 2009 it put sustainability at the heart of the Local Strategic Partnerships' (LSPs) Sustainable Community Strategy.

In summary, this period saw growth in the architecture for sustainable development and the mainstreaming of climate change. The SDC was created to bring sustainability into the heart of government; sustainable development plans were strengthened and underpinned by guiding principles; Defra became the lead department for sustainability; and DECC was created. The period also saw the emphasis narrow from sustainable development to focus particularly on climate change, highlighted by the creation of DECC.

At regional level there was a build up of structures: the Regional Development Agency in particular had a sustainable development remit. Government offices also played a role in negotiating Local Area Agreements (LAA) with local authorities. At local authority level, at its best Agenda 21 inspired a range of creative responses to the sustainability agenda until it was disbanded in 2007. After this there was a gap where momentum was lost, then a build up of duties from various modernisation initiatives to the point where sustainable development was viewed as almost a duty.

Coalition: 2010–present

2010 *Abolition of the regional tier of government, the SDC, the Sustainable Community Strategy and the Audit Commission.*

Plans for implementing a range of initiatives: these include expanding the Carbon Reduction Commitment Energy Efficiency Scheme (CRC); reform of the energy supply system to put intelligence into the system so the user can be much clearer about how energy is used and control it better; introduction of energy efficiency policies including the 'Green Deal', that is, to provide the money for insulating homes and create jobs; introduction of a floor price for carbon to regain investor confidence; expansion of Ofgem's (the energy regulator) role to account for climate change and energy security; and creation of the flagship 'Green Investment Bank' bringing financiers into government and hopefully unlocking money.

2011 *Energy Act 2011* (http://www.decc.gov.uk/en/content/cms/ legislation/energy_act2011/energy_act2011.aspx): including provisions for the new 'Green Deal' intended to reduce carbon emissions cost effectively by improving the energy efficiency of properties. The Green Deal financial mechanism eliminates the need to pay upfront for energy efficiency measures.

2012 *The UK Green Investment Bank formed as a public company*: with initial funding of £3 billion to March 2015. The status is as a company with an independent board operating at arm's length from Government, its sole initial shareholder. It is the world's first investment bank solely dedicated to greening the economy.

In summary, climate change is important to the Coalition Government. There is also quite a lot of cross-party support for tackling climate change, meaning that some legislation put in train by Labour was implemented by the Coalition. Examples include nuclear power stations and the CRC. However, as time passed splits in the Coalition became apparent. In 2012 Ed Davey replaced Chris Huhne as Energy Secretary and raised concerns of an 'anti-green' faction in the Tory party which felt that green policies such as investment in wind farms and solar power were too costly at a time of recession. The Coalition was also criticised for being poor on implementation. Examples include the Green Investment Bank not being allowed to borrow until 2015; the carbon floor price being set too low; and knocks to investor confidence by cuts in solar subsidies.

The impact of policy on local government is illustrated in the next chapter.

CHAPTER 4

Where Are We –
A Picture of Sustainability
in Local Government

Climate change is the best available single proxy we have for learning to live more sustainably, creating wealth more sustainably, etc.

(Jonathon Porritt)

TO ESTABLISH A PICTURE of sustainability in local government the author interviewed sustainability and climate change leads in nine local authorities across England, supported by leading sustainability advocates including Jonathon Porritt OBE, Ken Melamed (former mayor of Whistler, British Columbia, Canada) and award-winning charity Forum for the Future. The findings unveil rich insights into sustainable development in local government across four main areas:

Section 1: Perspectives on sustainable development

Section 2: The sustainability service

Section 3: The prominence of sustainable development

Section 4: Motivating and constraining factors to embedding sustainability.

These are detailed below under the respective questions. (Authorities and participants have not been listed by name to retain anonymity, quotes are in italics.)

SECTION 1:
Perspectives on sustainable development

Q1. How does the local authority define sustainable development?

The majority of authorities use a triple bottom line definition of sustainable development; a minority focus specifically on environmental sustainability. While understanding of sustainable development is increasing amongst staff and councillors, many are unsure what it means: 'it's quite muddy and you need to define what you mean'.

Councils with embedded sustainable development practices are more likely to have staff with a more developed understanding of the term due to the increased emphasis on training and capacity-building provided by these authorities. However, even here some stakeholders hold a narrow environmental perspective on sustainable development.

Finally, staff often view sustainability from the perspective of the role undertaken, therefore relating the term to the task is helpful when promoting sustainable development.

Q2. How helpful is the public value case in promoting sustainable development?

There is general acceptance of the argument that sustainability is the best framework on which to build public value; however, public value does not stimulate debate in the way that climate change or the efficiencies agenda do.

Q3. Where would you place the authority on the 'spectrum of public sector leadership on sustainable development?'

The spectrum used is published by Forum for the Future in their guide: 'Stepping up – Framework for Public Sector Leadership' (Birney et al, 2010). It has five levels of progress against which a local authority can assess itself; these levels are summarised as follows:

i. At risk: rare, but likely to breach legislative requirements.

ii. Compliance: understands legislative requirements and fulfils them.

iii. Incremental: takes sustainability more seriously but one of a number of competing priorities.

iv. Strategic: sustainable development is at the heart of strategy.

v. Systemic: sustainability is ingrained in the organisation's thinking, values, principles and planning.

The majority of authorities are at the 'incremental' stage, that is, they are taking sustainable development more seriously but it is still one of a number of competing priorities. Figure 7 provides an overview of authorities' positions against the five levels of the spectrum.

. . . .

FIGURE 7. Local authorities' position on the spectrum.

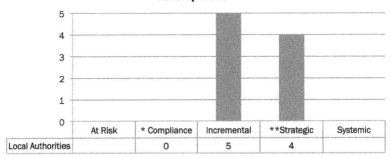

Local authorities positons on the
'Spectrum of public sector leadership in sustainable
development'

	At Risk	* Compliance	Incremental	**Strategic	Systemic
Local Authorities		0	5	4	

NOTE: Two of the 'Strategic' authorities felt they were on the verge of 'Systemic'.

. . . .

The spectrum provides a useful overview of where the authority is and where it needs to be on the path to ingraining sustainable development principles within the authority, with the following provisos:

- Local authorities are large organisations and many traditionally operate in silos, affording the likelihood that different parts of the organisation will be at different stages on the spectrum; therefore you have to give an overall rating.

- It is possible to go backwards on the spectrum if sustainability efforts are not sustained. For example, where an authority de-prioritises climate change their position can be expected to move backwards on the spectrum.

- Significant progress is required to move between the stages on the spectrum.

This final point is that while the majority position on the spectrum is 'Incremental' the range within this is large. It includes authorities where senior leadership has not adopted sustainable development as a priority, to authorities that are working on wide-ranging proposals to embed sustainability, but are not there yet.

SECTION 2:
The sustainability service

Q4. Does the authority have a dedicated sustainable development service? If so, what is it called and under which directorate is it situated?

Most authorities have a dedicated sustainability team of between three and eight staff; in light of spending cuts some are at risk – refer to question 12. A third of services are labelled 'Sustainability and Climate Change'. Authorities at the top end of the spectrum are more likely to have a named head of sustainability with sustainability functions intergraded into the directorate of approximately 40 staff. The lesson is that as authorities embed sustainability, functions are integrated into existing job roles with access to sustainability professionals. Specialist sustainability expertise is necessary for tasks such as monitoring, advising and initiating relevant new projects.

In the majority of cases the sustainability team reports within the Environment Directorate, frequently dealing with 'built environment' or 'place'. The second strong theme is regeneration, further evidenced by the significant proportion of sustainability managers with a town planning and regeneration background (see question 5).

The prominence of environment in locating sustainability services reflects both the history of sustainable development teams as well as the activities undertaken. Sustainability grew from environmental services, followed by Agenda 21 launched in 1992 and disbanded in 2007, and latterly picked up as part of the Sustainable Communities Strategy (SCS).

Q5. What is the background of the sustainable development service manager?

There is a strong correlation between the service manager's background and the main activities of the sustainability service. The dominant background of sustainability managers is environmental and activities of sustainability services are predominately environmentally focused. This is illustrated in Figure 8.

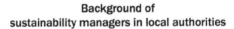

FIGURE 8. Background of sustainability managers.

Background of
sustainability managers in local authorities

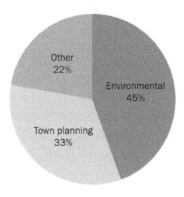

Other
22%

Environmental
45%

Town planning
33%

The location of sustainable development services, the title of services and the background of staff working within those services is related to the activities performed.

Q6. What are the authority's main sustainable development activities?

There are two main points: first, climate change activities are dominating the agenda; second, sustainable development activities are focused both internally and externally, as discussed below.

Activities are taking place in transport, planning, energy, properties, green spaces, regeneration, education, policy and research, environmental health and safety, and neighbourhood teams. Authorities clearly do have strong social (low educational attainment; high teenage pregnancy rates; low aspirations; deprivation, etc.) and economic (unemployment; regeneration; the green economy, etc.) focuses. However, the dominant focus is carbon reduction and climate change.

Most authorities have been targeting sustainable development activities both within the council itself and externally with wider stakeholders through strategic boards and partnership projects. In some areas the lead sustainability role is split into two posts: one promoting internal measures (culture change within the authority, capacity-building, internal waste and energy saving activities, etc.), the other working externally building stakeholder support. Examples include capacity-building with schools, businesses and the community, and promoting joint projects working on carbon reduction projects such as environmental construction, eco retro-fit programmes (up-grading energy efficiency through better insulation, lower energy consumption appliances, etc.), training for environmental jobs, and initiatives around feed-in tariffs (e.g. selling solar energy back to the national grid), etc. The bad news is early warnings suggest about a third of authorities are responding to funding cuts by dropping this external focus and limiting activities to reducing emissions on their estates (Scott, 2011).

Q7. Provide a brief history of the growth of the sustainable development service, including staff numbers.

In the period prior to and following the 2008 Climate Change Act there was significant activity in terms of growth of sustainable development functions. Services had increases in staff numbers, sometimes as a result of re-organisation and consolidation, in other cases due to recruitment to grow the service. The numbers, though small, are significant; for example, two authorities said that 'until three years ago one person dealt with all sustainability issues'. Now they both have sustainability teams of three or more staff. Increased sustainable development activity was reflected in leadership adopting sustainability as a priority issue, capacity-building and authorities producing sustainability action plans for the first time, generating the need for staff to effect implementation. This is not to detract from those authorities who have been committed to sustainability for many years; it is more a case of the remaining authorities joining in.

Public sector funding cuts suggest a less rosy picture is emerging. Faye Scott (2012) reveals a three-way split between local authorities with one third remaining firm in their commitment to climate change, one third narrowing their focus to reducing emissions on their own estates and the final third de-prioritising climate change functions.

Q8. How is sustainable development funded?

Sustainability teams are mainly core funded, though increasingly teams are having to fight for budgets and in some areas supplement this with funding applications. Units deliver revenue savings and/or generation projects; the majority generate small amounts of income; however, a few generate significant amounts. There are three main ways of generating or saving income:

1. *Efficiency savings*: this has become a high priority. All authorities are undertaking eco retro-fits (up-grading energy efficiency through better insulation, lower energy consumption appliances, etc.) to varying degrees. Investment frequently depends on anticipated returns; some authorities use formulas for working out the expected return on investment. The Carbon Trust advises that efficiency measures in buildings can be expected to achieve savings in the range of 5–10%.

2. *Projects*: authorities are involved in sustainable projects; the more ingrained sustainable development is in the authority, the greater the focus on this. Consultancy budgets are used to commission work or facilitate partnerships to strengthen funding bids for joint projects.

3. *Delivering services*: examples include purchasing energy and undertaking energy assessments. Since April 2011 local authorities have been allowed to generate income from renewable energy.

In addition to the above, refer to question 13 on the effects of the current economic crisis.

SECTION 3:
Prominence of sustainable development

Q9. Where does leadership for sustainable development come from within the authority?

In 2008 the SDC report 'Capability for Local Sustainability' noted that in the majority of cases the manager of the sustainability service led on the agenda within the authority. This has since changed. Of the nine authorities interviewed, in two-thirds of cases leadership comes from the top (see Figure 9).

....

FIGURE 9. Leadership of the sustainability agenda.

Leadership of the sustainability agenda in local authorities

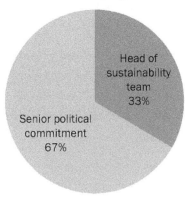

Head of sustainability team 33%

Senior political commitment 67%

....

The importance of senior commitment to embedding sustainability is both intuitive and reflected by several authors. Dan McCartney (2010) suggests that five themes dictate a council's ability to affect area wide emissions, the first of which is political and organisation commitment (others included: finance; local citizen engagement; partnership working; and staff and skills capacity). Interview findings supported McCartney's assessment of the significance of senior commitment: 'Having committed leadership opens access to resources and facilitates progress irrespective of any barriers.'

Q10. What capacity-building activities are undertaken for sustainable development, e.g. training, development, support, etc.?

Building capacity in sustainable development ranges from ad hoc presentations to sustainability being embedded in job descriptions and development programmes. Even though only a few authorities have achieved the latter, sustainability managers are aiming for the latter.

Capacity-building programmes include networking, giving presentations and awareness-raising. Sustainability staff have often been trained in influencing skills. As well as internal activities, authorities are involved in a range of external capacity-building activities (refer to question 6). All authorities undertake community consultations; responses to these provide impetus for pursuing sustainability objectives.

The Municipality of Whistler in British Columbia is one of the Canada's leaders in community sustainability planning, engagement and imple-mentation. Ken Melamed, past mayor of Whistler, recommends authorities tackle the lack of understanding of sustainable development (identified in question 1) and that capacity is built to gain confidence and commitment. The programme they used involved community awareness and learning initiatives, including: train-the-trainer workshops teaching stakeholders to deliver sustainability awareness presentations; training courses; sustainability symposiums; a community speaker series; and a community engagement programme including workshops, booklets, and other resources for householders, businesses and schools. The story of Whistler, BC, can be accessed here: http://www.ecotippingpoints.org/our-stories/indepth/canada-whistler-sustainable-community-planning.html.

Q11. Are sustainability tools (e.g. lifecycle cost analysis and accreditations such as ISO 14001) used to promote and develop sustainable approaches to strategy and policy?

Local authorities do use sustainability tools. The points to bear in mind are:

- Sustainability tools are useful in getting authorities started with sustainability. Once practices become more ingrained the need for them lessens.

- Financial pressures have driven some authorities to discontinue relevant accreditations, such as ISO 14001 accreditation. (ISO 14001 is an internationally accepted standard that sets out how to put in place an effective Environmental Management System or EMS.)

- Tools need to be proportional and practical, that is, not add significant burden or cost.

- Life cycle costing has been adopted or is being considered in the majority of authorities. (Life cycle costing [LCC], also called whole life costing, is a technique to establish the total cost of ownership. It is a structured approach that addresses all the elements of this cost and can be used to produce a spend profile of the product or service over its anticipated lifespan.)

There are significant gains to be made in terms of lowering carbon emissions through sustainable procurement. One Defra report states that 77% of the greenhouse gas emissions making up the carbon footprint of central government come from the supply chain. Likewise, the Carbon Disclosure Project's 2012 supply chain report suggests that 'scope 3' emissions (indirect emissions from outsourced operations, business travel in vehicles not owned by the company, embodied energy in products purchased, waste disposal) account for as much as 86% of a business's carbon footprint.

Q12. What are the effects of the current economic climate, if any?

The recession and cuts in authorities' budgets are having both negative and positive effects. Positive effects include:

- The emphasis being put on financial savings has moved sustainability up the political agenda; efficiency drives not necessarily motivated from a sustainability perspective are nonetheless reducing resource use. Examples include: the adoption of widespread home-working practices (the cost of office space in Britain is the highest in the world); the selling off of energy inefficient buildings (the buildings will still be there and unless the new owners undertake eco upgrades, relatively high emissions remain) and building adaptation measures.

- Greater willingness to pursue ideas – local energy generation is a popular example.

- An opportunity to come out of recession with a low-carbon dimension achieved through behaviour change.

- Growth of the green economy and opportunities from this, for example, sustainable construction (for growth areas, refer to BIS, 2009).

- An increasing trend to include sustainability targets and indicators in key plans; as one authority explained 'if it's not measured you won't get funding for it'.

Negative effects are:

- Vulnerability of the service in light of budget cuts. Previously noted are fears that a third of local authorities could drop the service altogether and of the remaining two-thirds, 50% may be reducing their function to mainly focus on carbon reduction within their internal estates.

- Lower budgets affecting consultants and partnership working which in turn affects the strength of funding applications, accreditation, capacity-building and sustainability tools.

- Increased significance of short-term returns from efficiency investments, thus threatening some investment. Additionally, there is uncertainty as to what will happen if forecasted financial savings from efficiency measures come in at below projected levels.

SECTION 4:
Motivating and constraining factors
to embedding sustainability

Q13. What factors are most likely to be influential in encouraging local authorities to adopt sustainability practices?

There are a range of motivations behind the adoption of sustainable development within local government. It is difficult to select a single factor, as one authority put it 'this is not a single item agenda'. However, four recurring themes are:

1. **Government**: central government is influential particularly in respect of local government and it is important that they send out the right signals.

2. **Personal conviction of leaders**: the significance of leaders driving the agenda forward should not be underestimated. The key is to ingrain sustainability practice so that a change of personnel or administration does not impact on this commitment.

3. **Financial savings**: a significant motivator for all authorities.

4. **Business case**: as one interviewee said, 'it's about keeping in profit'. To stay in business local councils need 'places' to be attractive and economically prosperous so that they are desirable; to compete they need to be efficient; and they need to be able to adapt to climate change. 'Environmental sustainability is about good business, the best of the private sector already recognise this.'

All these motivations support the case for adapting to sustainable practices. Using just one example as an illustration: changing to sustainable transport raises air quality, reduces congestion and road wear and reduces carbon emissions. The area is made more attractive to residents, which supports economic prosperity, the authority benefits from the economic prosperity and savings from reduced road wear – in a long view, a virtuous circle.

A fuller list of motivating factors and brief explanation is provided in the table below:

Influential factors in encouraging the adoption of sustainable practices

Government, including legislation and assessments: examples include: the Climate Change Act, government as a role model, guidance and assessments: 'Managers serve the needs of whatever they are being assessed on.'

Party politics: the Green Party and the Liberal Democrats are traditionally viewed as most progressive in this area.

Electorate/residents/local interest groups: most authorities annually survey residents to find out what is important to them; this is influential when deciding on local priorities. Additionally local pressure groups can be important in shaping the local agenda.

Personal conviction: authorities with a tradition of sustainability had commonly started due to the personal conviction of prominent figures; in one area the Finance Director had been a keen environmentalist and was key in driving the agenda forward; in another it was the Planning Officer.

Financial savings: reducing cost is a priority issue in all authorities.

Business case: to attract industry and talent authorities have to make their area a nice place to live and work – being unspoilt is an increasingly important factor. Authorities also have to make the books balance; therefore, they need to cut unnecessary wastage, generate income, and attract funding where they can.

Public service ethos: the public value case (refer to Chapter 3).

Learning from the private sector: one practice undertaken is to look at carbon cutting measures being taken in the private sector with a view to adopting suitable measures.

Peer pressure/being seen as leaders: peer pressure is more of an issue in London where authorities are located close together and regularly meet at events; additionally proximity to national MPs has an effect. Being seen as leaders is the more important factor outside of London.

Q14. Is it more difficult for the public sector to ingrain sustainability into the heart of strategy than for the private sector, and if so, what unique barriers do they face?

The complexity and diversity of government is the biggest barrier to sustainable development. The activities, stakeholders, regulations, structures and mechanisms of government are all complex. A compilation of barriers is provided in the table below.

Barriers to sustainable development in local authorities

Complex and diverse range of activities: 'The public sector is fundamentally more complex.' 'You would be hard pressed to find a private sector organisation that has to deliver the range of services within the same financial pressures... It's a big ship... you cannot turn it around quickly.'

Large, complex, and diverse range of stakeholders: these include, for example, the full range of professions each with their own professional institutions and standards, local groups, government edicts, political expectations and the public service ethos.

Bureaucratic and complex structures: one challenge is understanding the plethora of structures, the other is working within them and the restrictions they impose.

Time horizons and short-sightedness: the short-term nature of elected positions makes it very difficult for leaders to make real progress on longer-term priorities like sustainable development. Jonathon Porritt notes one authority where councillors were elected every year.

Competition for and lack of resources: where sustainability is not an organising principle of government, it competes with many different priorities. Lack of resources is currently particularly prevalent.

Answerable to the political agenda: 'local government is restricted and cannot make a decision in the way that the private sector can'.

Heavily regulated: 'very few authorities actually have the power to make things happen and work with their own communities to get faster processes of change going. It's very stuck' (Jonathon Porritt). 'Government mechanisms and compliance work does not lend itself to creative ways of working – even though there is a lot of appetite for it.'

Lack of competition in the public sector: 'Residents cannot choose who empties their bins; therefore they do not have the same incentives.'

Climate sceptics: there are plenty of stakeholders who do not believe in climate change.

Difficult to implement: 'to deliver sustainable outcomes you need sustainable processes, the way you do business becomes important, you have to move from operating silos to a holistic model. This is difficult.'

The aim of this chapter was to establish a picture of sustainability in local government and uncover key insights for ingraining sustainability in the public sector. What follows is a brief summary followed by three crucial ingredients for embedding sustainability.

The picture in local government is one of sizable differences between authorities in respect of the progress made to embed sustainability. With the Climate Change Act on the horizon significant growth and development took place including: the formulation of sustainable development teams through re-organisation or recruitment; increased communication of sustainability; action or visioning to incorporate sustainability into job descriptions and staff and member development programmes; and the creation of Climate Change Panels. Progress to embed sustainability, in some areas, is now being lost following the effects of drastic cuts to local authority budgets.

The primary focus of activities is environmental, with climate change and carbon reduction topping the agenda. Activities supporting sustainable development are taking place across local authority departments from Property to Planning. Sustainability teams provide expert advice and are involved with income-generating projects, a minority of which generate significant amounts. Savings are also being created from resource efficiency; some teams/staff are funded on the basis of projected savings.

In authorities where sustainability is more ingrained into practice, a key motivating factor has commonly been committed and influential individuals (leaders) being able to drive sustainability practices forward within the authority. Mainstreaming sustainability practice is essential to ensure that progress is not lost when key individuals or political administrations change.

In terms of cutting emissions, sustainable procurement has the potential to contribute the largest gains to carbon reduction; however, it is generally a less well developed area. At the opposite end of the spectrum, the range and complexity of services, structures and stakeholders in local government is the most commonly cited reason for the gap in progress made between the best of the private sector and local government.

Local authorities did not know how the carbon reduction targets for 2050 would be met stating that current activities are insufficient to achieve this commitment. The next and final chapter introduces the mechanisms being used to meet legislative carbon reduction targets. A number of drivers enabling sustainability in local government emerged, the three most significant are detailed below.

- Whilst awareness of sustainable development was increasing amongst staff, councillors and stakeholders, *many were unsure what it meant*. In which case the single most important action needed is to build a widespread grounding in basic sustainability understanding across each local authority. This in turn will help to develop motivation for urgent action through a better understanding of the damage being caused by current unsustainable practices.

- *Personal conviction of leaders* was a prominent factor in a high percentage of authorities who had embedded sustainability. As one local authority sustainability manager put it, 'Having committed leadership opens access to resource and facilitates progress irrespective of any barriers.'

- The third critical factor is *sustainable procurement*. There are big gains to be made in terms of lowering carbon emissions from sustainable procurement. CDP's 2012 supply chain report suggests that 'scope 3' emissions account for as much as 86% of a business's carbon footprint, whilst a Defra report suggests that 77% of the greenhouse gas emissions making up the carbon footprint of central government come from the supply chain.

CHAPTER 5

What Next?

Current activities will not lead to the achievement of the 80% reduction in emissions by 2050. No authority knows how the carbon reduction target of 80% will be achieved.

(Local Authority Sustainability and Climate Change Team Leader)

CHAPTER 4 PROVIDED RICH INSIGHTS on sustainability in local government. Prior to funding cuts sustainability functions in local government were growing, with tackling climate change being the primary focus. However, the point was made that, 'No authority knows how the carbon reduction target of 80% will be achieved.' In this final chapter the aim is to build an understanding of the mechanisms through which the UK government plans to achieve the greenhouse gas (GHG) emissions targets, and the role of the public sector in these.

How will the UK achieve the carbon reduction targets? The primary vehicles for achieving these targets are the European Union Emissions Trading Scheme (EU ETS) and the Carbon Reduction Commitment Energy Efficiency Scheme (CRC). These schemes are discussed below, along with carbon reduction policies aimed at small and medium-sized enterprises (SMEs) and consumers.

European Union Emissions Trading Scheme (EU ETS)

In 2005 the Kyoto Protocol came into force. Under the Kyoto Protocol, industrialised countries and the European Community committed to reducing emissions of greenhouse gases. The European Communities method for achieving this was to introduce the European Union Emissions Trading Scheme.

The EU ETS was the first international organisation-level system of allowances for emitting carbon dioxide (CO_2) and other greenhouse gases. The scheme works on the 'cap and trade' principle which means there is a 'cap' or limit, on the total amount of certain greenhouse gases that can be emitted by the organisations in the system. Within this cap, organisations receive emission allowances. At the end of each year each organisation must surrender enough allowances to cover all its emissions, otherwise fines are imposed. If an organisation reduces its emissions, it can keep the spare allowances to cover its future needs or sell them to another company that is short of allowances. The flexibility that trading brings ensures that emissions are cut where it costs least to do so. The number of allowances is reduced over time so that total emissions fall. In 2020 emissions will be 21% lower than in 2005.

The EU ETS covers electricity generation and the main energy-intensive industries including power stations, refineries and offshore rigs, iron and steel, cement and lime, paper, food and drink, glass, ceramics, engineering and the manufacture of vehicles. Direct effects of the EU ETS on the public sector are limited. The main impact is through indirect costs from increased charges for goods and services to both the public sector body and the communities they service. Direct impacts on the public sector are channelled through the CRC Energy Efficiency Scheme.

Carbon Reduction Commitment Energy Efficiency Scheme (CRC)

The UK 2008 Climate Change Act imposed legally binding reductions on CO_2 emissions. As of 2013 the EU ETS, aimed at energy intensive industries, covers about 48% of UK national CO_2 emissions and is the principal system for achieving these targets. Large public and private sector organisations not covered by the EU ETS fall within the catchment of the (mandatory) Carbon Reduction Commitment Energy Efficiency Scheme. Organisations covered by the CRC have to measure and report their emissions, which are mostly the result of gas and electricity use, and pay per tonne for the CO_2 they produce.

With the CRC and EU ETS covering the energy intensive industries and large public and private sector organisations, that leaves small- and medium-sized enterprises (SMEs) and the general public. Needless to say this segment has not been forgotten – rafts of policies are aimed at this sector and the main ones are outlined below.

Carbon reduction policies for SMEs and consumers

The government has focused on developing a range of consumer facing policies that will support SMEs and householders in reducing their energy use. These include:

- *Electricity micro-generation feed-in-tariff (FiT)*: upon the installation of micro-generators, such as solar panels, the FiT pays householders for every unit of renewable electricity generated (up to 5 MW) and gives additional payments for every unit exported back to the grid. Generating their own energy, the householder also benefits from reduced energy bills. Anyone wishing to install solar PV has to prove that their building has an energy efficiency rating of D or above.

- *Household Renewable Heat Incentive (RHI) and Renewable Heat Premium Payment (RHPP)*: the domestic RHI will be available from summer 2013. Upon installation of a renewable heat device, such as a heat pump, householders will get a payment for every unit of renewable heat they generate. Prior to its introduction, the RHPP enables householders to get a grant towards the cost of installing renewable heat measures.

- *Green Deal*: aimed at encouraging the energy efficiency retrofit of homes by overcoming the financial barrier of having to pay for measures upfront. Householders are able to get energy efficiency measures installed via a Green Deal provider and pay back the cost through a charge on their electricity bill. The loans are attached to the property, so when occupancy changes the loan responsibility is passed to the new occupant.

- *Energy Company Obligation (ECO)*: a levy on household fuel bills provides a pot of money used to subsidise energy efficiency installations in properties not eligible for financing under the Green Deal, for example, because they are hard to treat. Half of this money is distributed by energy companies and half by other organisations who bid for a proportion.

- *Smart meter roll-out*: this will provide every home in the country with a smart meter that can read real time energy use by 2019. It will be supplier led and therefore delivered by energy companies according to the pattern and timetable that they see fit for their customers. The meters should provide customers with more accurate bills. Display units will enable people to see their real time use of electricity and gas, and they will receive energy efficiency advice from installers.

All of these schemes encourage changes in behaviour, or changes to the fabric or source of energy of properties, with the objectives of reducing carbon emissions, tackling fuel poverty and improving energy security. Local government's role in contributing to these and other climate change measures was recognised in a Memorandum of Understanding (MOU) in 2011 between DECC and the Local Government Group (http://www.local.gov.uk/). In this, MOU parties will work together to help and encourage all councils to take firm action to:

- reduce the carbon emissions from their own estate and operations;

- reduce carbon emissions from homes, businesses and transport infrastructure, creating more appropriate renewable energy generation, using council influence and powers; and

- participate in national carbon reduction initiatives at the local level, particularly the roll-out of the Green Deal, smart metering and renewable energy deployment.

The MOU recognises how councils, through local governance, can ensure climate change policies and programmes protect and help the most vulnerable, particularly the fuel poor. Policies set at national level affect the ability of councils to act at local level, and local action affects the ability of national government to meet its targets.

Now that the mechanisms for facilitating the UK's achievement of the 80% carbon reduction target have been revealed, and the role of local government in contributing to these has been exposed, the question is – are they making an impact?

Well, yes they are. Starting with the EU ETS, this scheme is now a cornerstone of the European Union's policy to combat climate change and by 2020 it will be the biggest single policy instrument for addressing climate change in the EU. The UK government expects the EU ETS to deliver *two-thirds* of the first three carbon budgets under the Climate Change Act 2008. A 'carbon budget' is a cap on the total quantity of greenhouse gas emissions emitted in the UK over a specified time. Each carbon budget covers a five-year period. The first three carbon budgets cover the following years: 2008–2012, 2013–2017, 2018–2022.

Moving on to consider the CRC, preparation for this has boosted awareness of energy efficiency; senior management of some large organisations are taking notice of energy bills for the first time. It has enabled carbon and energy-related officers to have an open dialogue with finance and resource teams in new ways, as there was little incentive to do so in the past. The CRC is boosting demand for energy efficiency goods and services, such as voltage optimisation equipment (a technology which reduces the voltages received by energy consumers in order to reduce energy use). The Environment Agency estimates that up to 11.6 million tonnes of carbon dioxide emissions per year could potentially be avoided by 2020 from sectors included in the CRC. Organisations can achieve this with overall cost savings or no net financial cost to participants as initial costs are offset by reduced energy bills. This would result in emissions reduction from this sector of around 28% from 1990 levels.

However the CRC is under threat. Following strong criticism that the scheme is too complicated, the government undertook a consultation on proposals to simplify the scheme resulting in an announcement in Dec 2012 that the league table, which ranks the relative emissions performance of firms, is to be abolished and the number of fuels that participants have to report on reduced from 29 to just two (electricity and gas for heating). The government also noted that a full review of the CRC will take place in 2016 and the tax element (the significant lever for driving down emissions) will be a high priority for removal when public finances allow. Instead the government is consulting on a financial incentive mechanism to actively encourage corporate energy efficiency (http://www.decc.gov.uk/en/content/cms/consultations/edr_cons/edr_cons.aspx) and, in April 2013, mandatory GHG emissions reporting (http://www.verdantix.com/index.cfm/papers/Products.Details/product_id/433/sustainability-reporting-frameworks-gain-global-traction/-) will arrive for the 1,800 largest listed firms in the UK. So while this may be the beginning of the end for the CRC, the wider policy landscape signals ongoing emphasis on encouraging corporate energy efficiency.

Carbon reduction policies targeting consumers and SMEs may prove to be tougher going. The rate of uptake needed to meet government targets is ambitious. It requires one home a minute to upgrade its energy efficiency between now and 2050, just under two homes an hour to install renewable heat between now and 2020 and ten homes a minute to have smart meters installed between 2014 and 2019. Achieving this will depend on the public actively engaging with the schemes and taking action, which for some of the initiatives includes spending their own money. The public also has to be made aware of the schemes and trust what they are being sold. The Green Deal could be a hard sell.

Clearly, we won't know until closer to 2050 if the UK carbon reduction targets are going to be achieved, however, we have travelled a long way. By putting a price on each tonne of carbon emitted, the CRC and EU ETS have forced the cost of emissions onto the agenda. Rising fuel costs and options from carbon reduction initiatives will also motivate SMEs and consumers to save energy. These schemes are also accredited with driving ingenuity, investment in low-carbon technologies and spawning a host of related new service sectors such as carbon trading, carbon finance, carbon management and carbon auditing.

....

Bibliography

Secondary sources

Giddens, A., Latham, S. and Liddle, R. (eds) 2009. *Building a Low-carbon future: The Politics of Climate Change* (London: Policy Network).

Birney, A., Clarkson, H., Madden, P., Porritt, J. and Tuxworth, B. 2010. *Stepping Up – A Framework for Public Sector Leadership* (London: Forum for the Future).

Carson, R. 1962. *Silent Spring* (Cambridge: Hamish Hamilton).

Cowe, R. and Porritt, J. 2002. *Government's Business: Enabling Corporate Sustainability* (London: Forum for the Future).

Dyllick, T. and Hockerts, K. 2002. Beyond the case for corporate sustainability. *Business Strategy and The Environment* (Volume 11 Issue 2): 130–141 (John Wiley & Sons Ltd and EPR Environment).

Grayson, D. 2010. United Kingdom. In Visser, W., and Tolhurst, N. (ed) *The World Guide to CSR, A Country-by-Country Analysis of Corporate Sustainability and Responsibility* (Sheffield: Greenleaf Publishing).

Jackson, T. 2009. *Prosperity Without Growth? The Transition to a Sustainable Economy* (London: Earthscan).

Matthes, F.C. 2009. Do we need the return of state planning to overcome the climate change challenge? In Giddens, A., Latham, S. and Liddle, R.

(eds) *Building a Low-carbon Future: The Politics of Climate Change* (London: Policy Network).

Parkin, S. 2010. *The Positive Deviant: Sustainability Leadership in a Perverse World* (London: Earthscan), Chapter 1, pp 17–46.

Phillips, R. and Scott, F. 2012. *Neither Sermons Nor Silence: The Case for National Communications on Energy Use* (London: Green Alliance).

Porritt, J. 2009. *The Standing of Sustainable Development in Government* (London: Forum for the Future).

Prugh, T., Constanza, R. and Daly, H. 2000. *The Local Politics of Global Sustainability* (Washington, DC: Island Press).

Scott, F. 2011. *Is Localism Delivering for Climate Change* (London: Green Alliance).

Shiva, V. 2002. *Staying Alive: Women, Ecology and Development* (London: Zen Books).

Stern, N. 2007. *The Economics of Climate Change: The Stern Review* (Cambridge: Cambridge University Press).

Primary sources

BIS. 2009. *Low Carbon and Environmental Goods and Services: An Industry Analysis, Update for 2008/9* (London: BIS, Department for Business Innovation and Skills).

Brundtland Commission.1989. *Our Common Future* (Oxford University Press)

HM Government. 2005. *Executive Summary: Securing the Future, Delivering UK Sustainable Development Strategy* (London: HM Government).

HM Government. 2005. *One Future – Different Paths. The UK's Shared Framework for Sustainable Development* (London: HM Government).

Kelly, G., Mulgan, G. and Muers, S. 2002. *Creating Public Value: An Analytical Framework for Public Service Reform* (London: Strategy Unit, Cabinet Office).

Welsh Assembly Government. 2009. *One Wales: One Planet* (Cardiff: Welsh Assembly Government).

Internet accessed sources

Carbon dioxide emissions by country, http://rainforests.mongabay.com/09

Stern Report Update: **http://www.knowledge.allianz.com/environment/ climate_change/?463/climate-change-costs-stern-review-update**

Earth Observatory, The Carbon Cycle: **http://earthobservatory.nasa. gov/Features/CarbonCycle/**

McCartney, D. 2010. A successful approach to climate change. Local Government Improvement and Development: **http://sitetest.idea.gov. uk/idk/core/page.do?pageId=19625911**

Poulter, S. and Derbyshire, D (2008): **http://www.thisismoney.co.uk/ money/bills/article-1620909/Banish-plastic-bags.html**

Rees, M. 2010. Rees Lectures: Surviving the century. *Scientific Horizons*, 8 June 2010, BBC Radio 4: http://www.bbc.co.uk/radio4/features/the-reecelectures/transcripts/2010

BIBLIOGRAPHY

World Bank Development Research Group, 2012: **http://go.worldbank. org/VL7N3V6F20**

....

For Product Safety Concerns and Information please contact our EU
representative GPSR@taylorandfrancis.com
Taylor & Francis Verlag GmbH, Kaufingerstraße 24, 80331 München, Germany

www.ingramcontent.com/pod-product-compliance
Ingram Content Group UK Ltd.
Pitfield, Milton Keynes, MK11 3LW, UK
UKHW040928180425
457613UK00011B/291